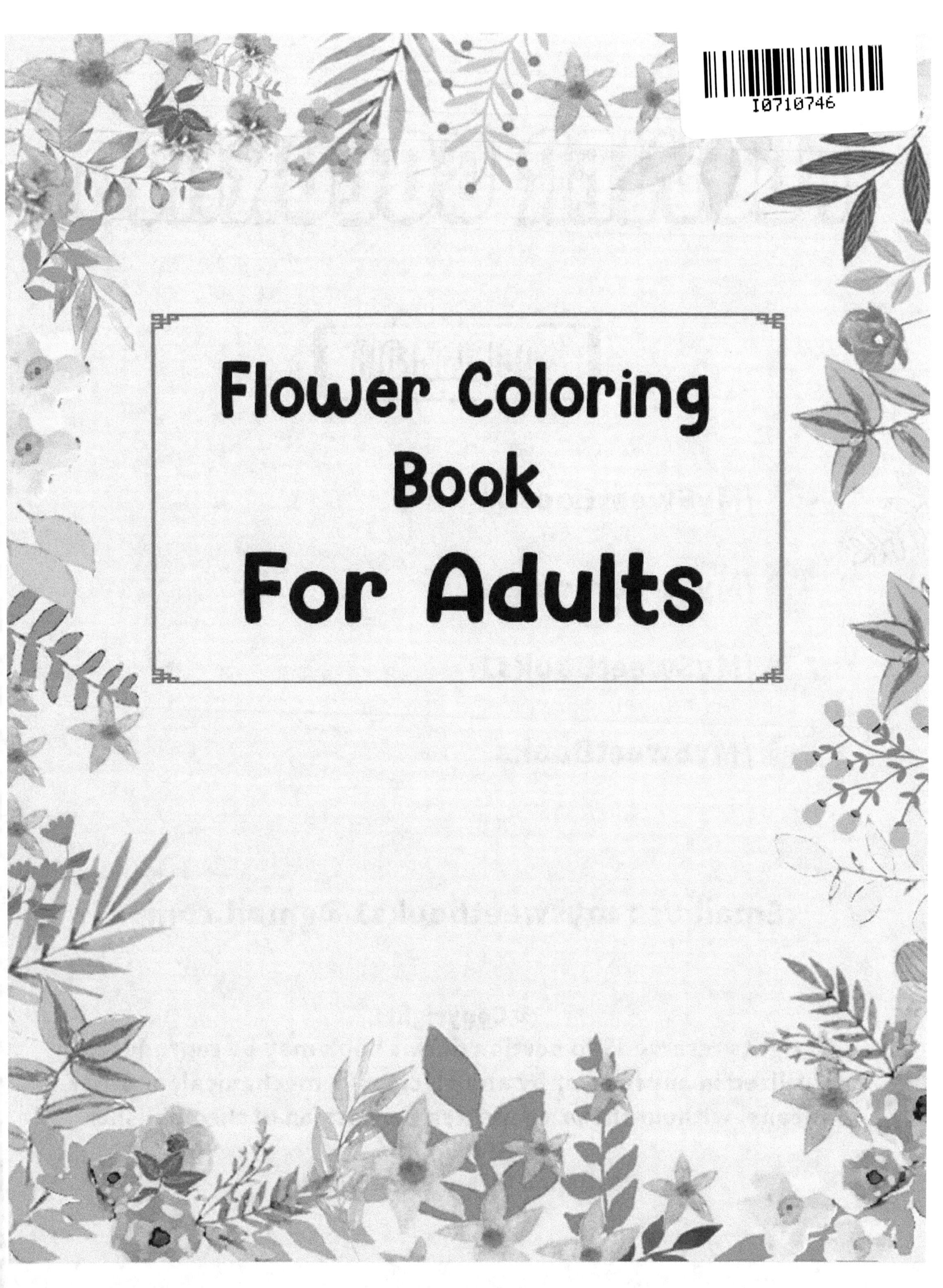
Flower Coloring
Book
For Adults

FLOWER COLORING

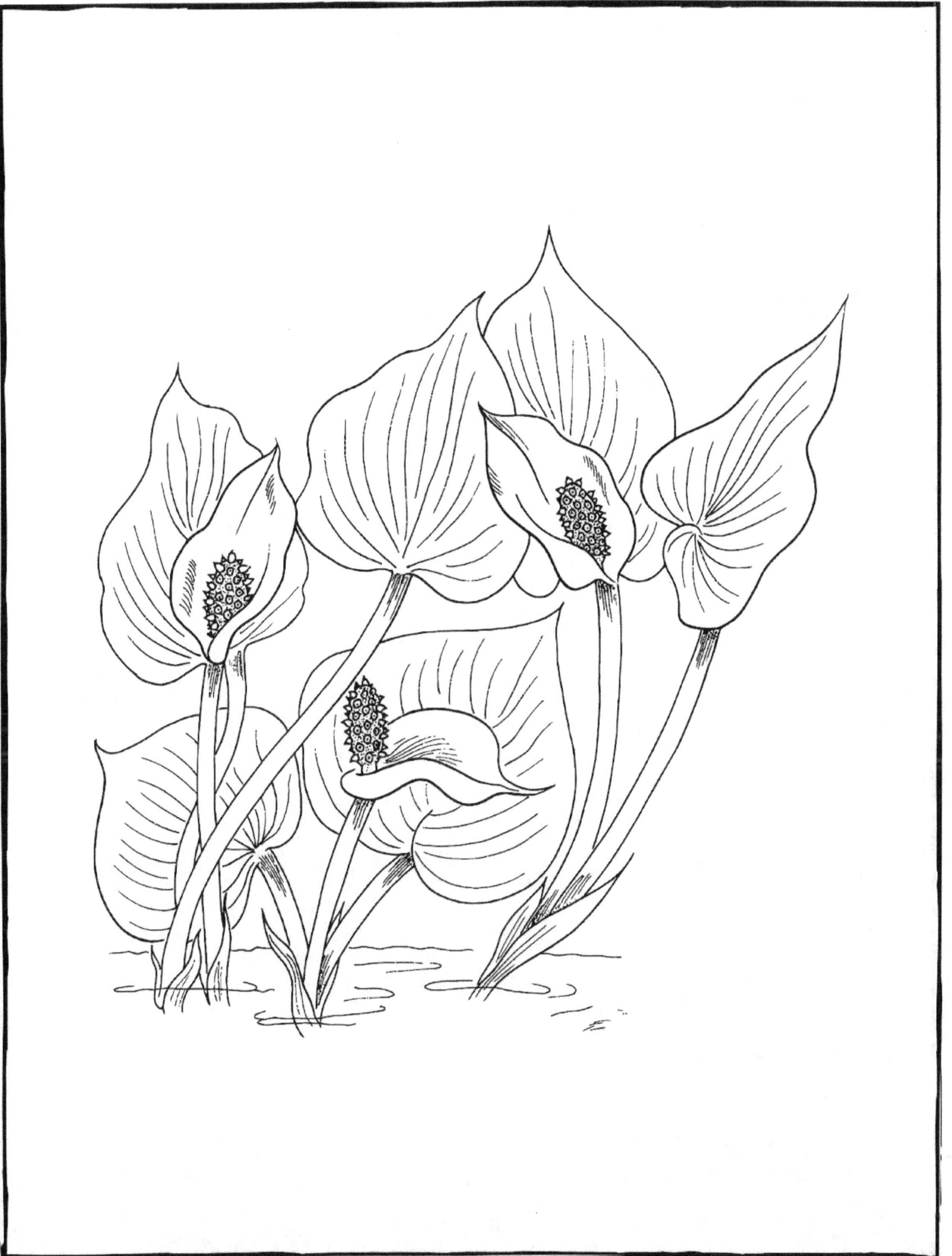

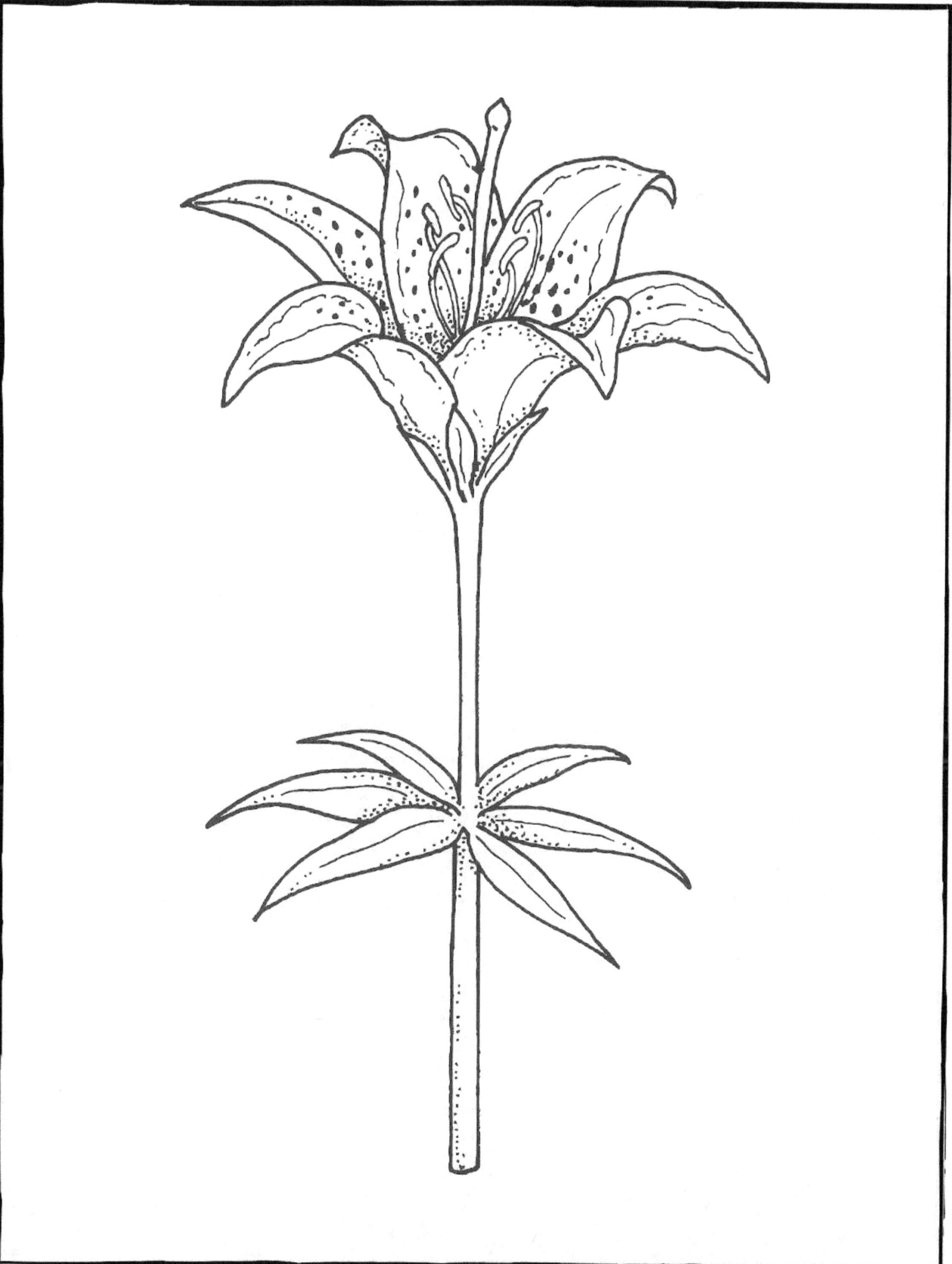

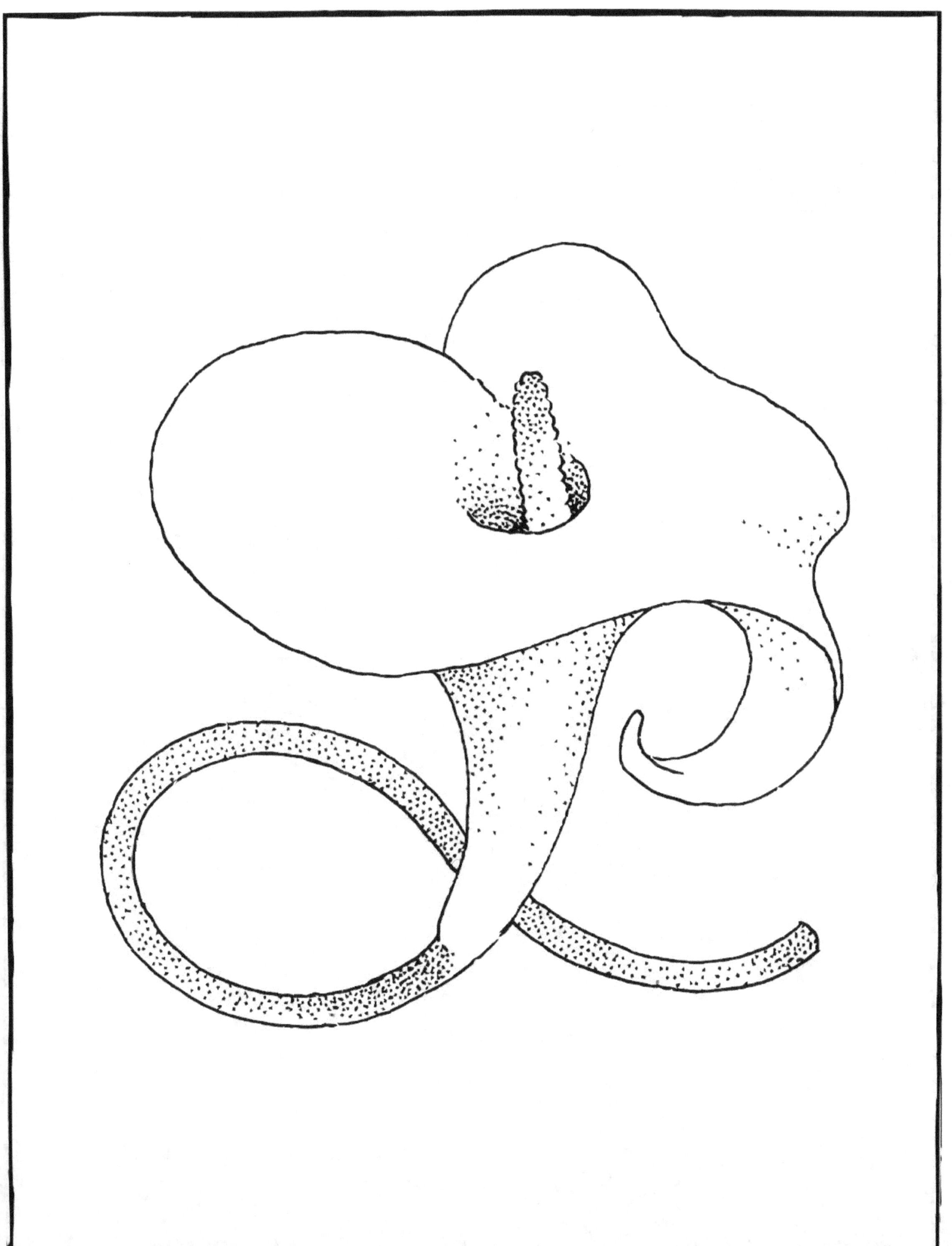

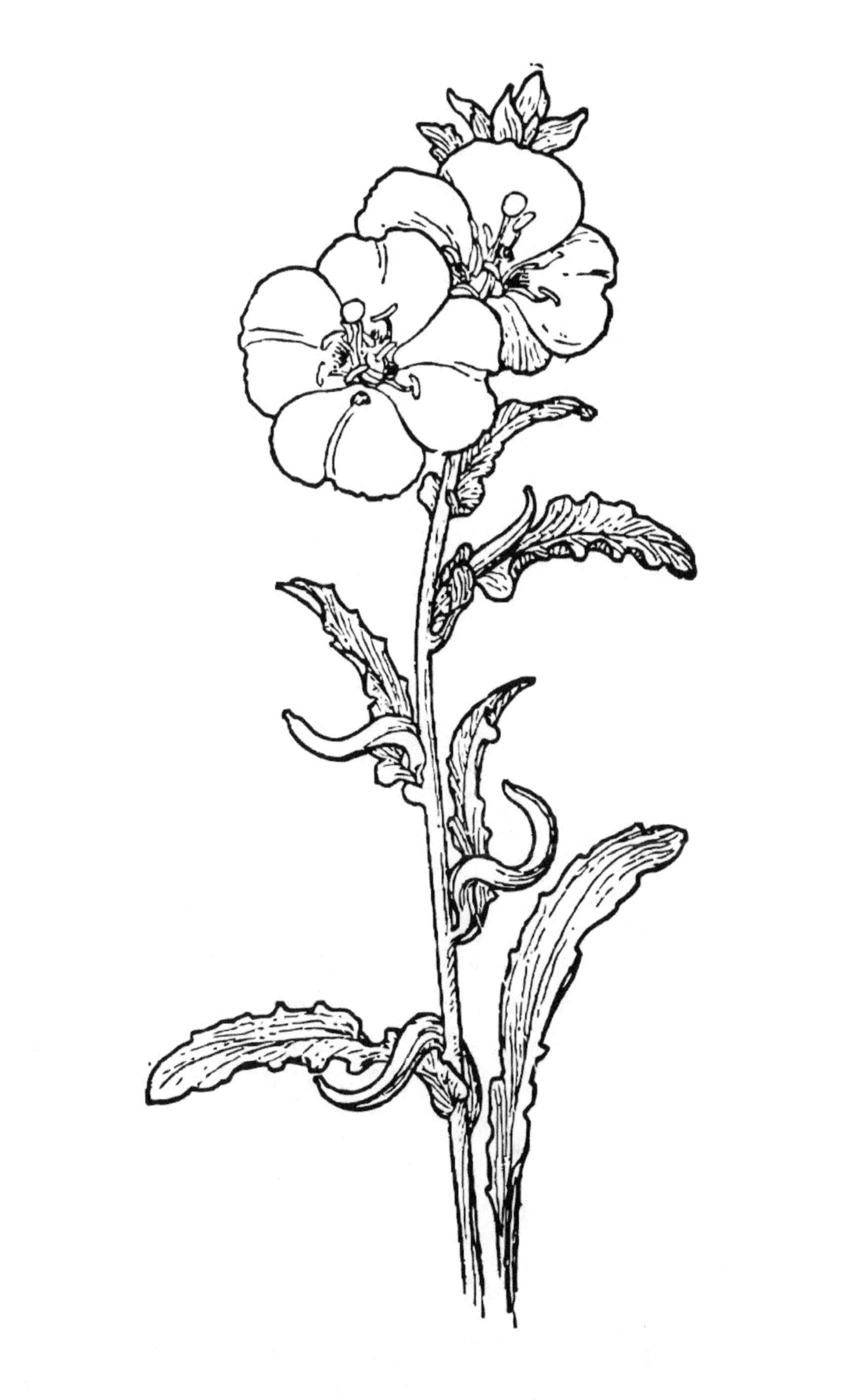

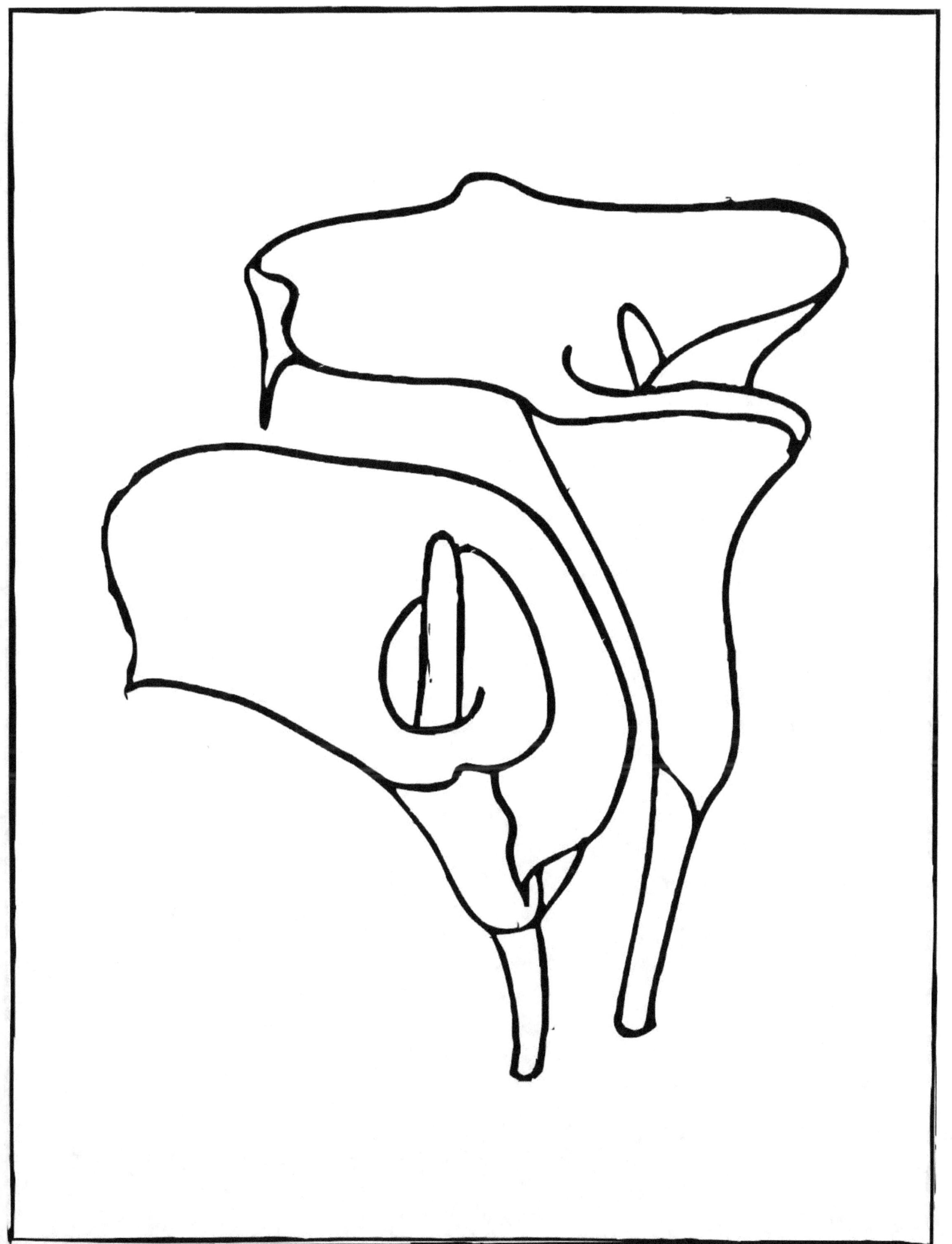

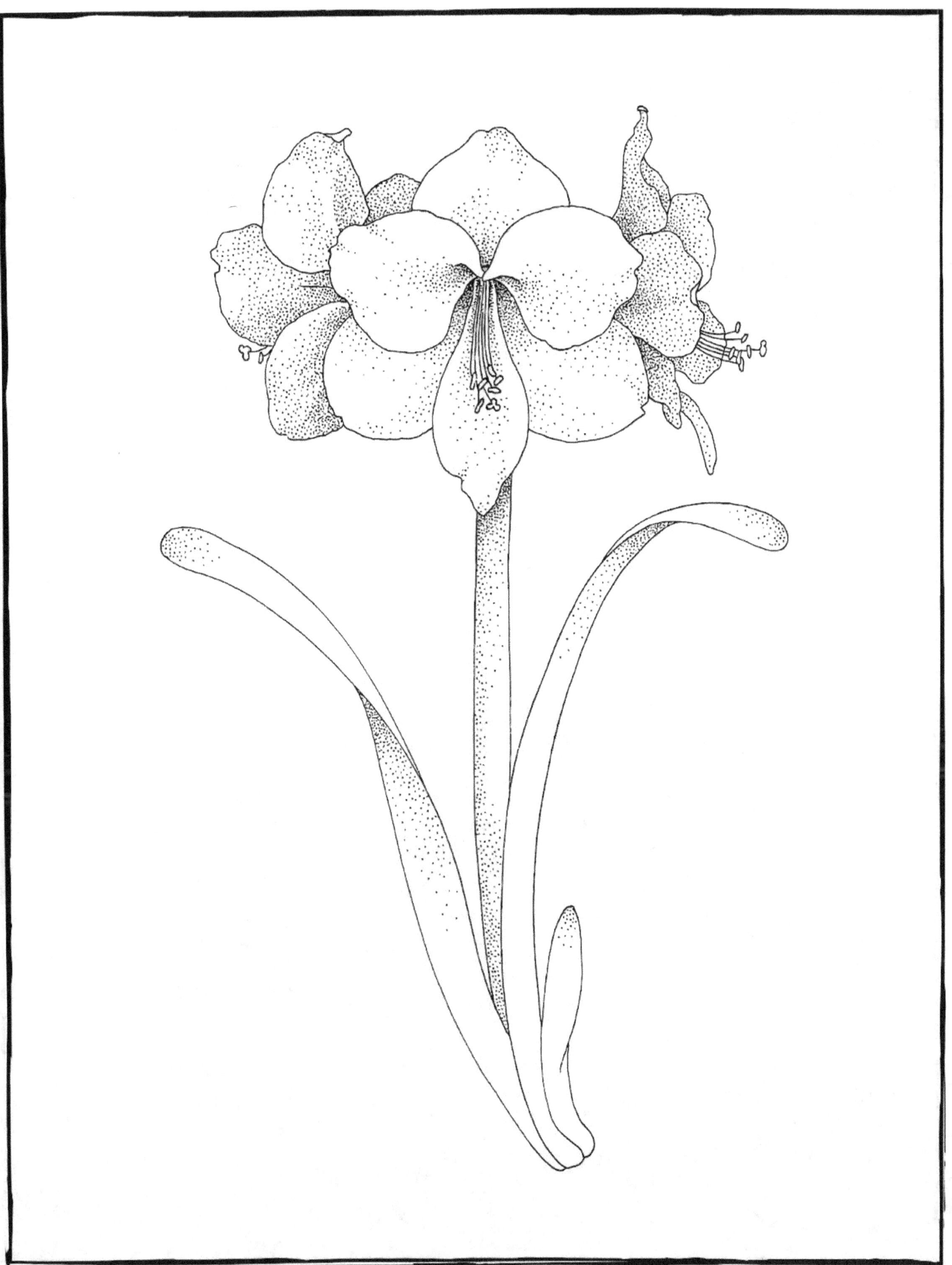